TERENCE MUNSEY

How To:

BE A PUBLISHED AUTHOR

MUNSEY MUSIC
TORONTO LOS ANGELES LONDON

HOW TO: BE A PUBLISHED AUTHOR
PUBLISHED BY
MUNSEY MUSIC
BOX 511, RICHMOND HILL, ONTARIO, CANADA, L4C 4Y8
FAX: 905 737 0208
E-MAIL: munsey@pathcom.com
WEBSITE: www.pathcom.com/~munsey

Canadian Cataloguing in Publication Data
Munsey, Terence, 1953-
How to: be a published author
ISBN 0-9685152-0-7
I. Self-publishing. 2. Authorship. I. Title.
Z285.5.M86 2000 070.5'93 C99-932005-X

Library of Congress Catalogue Number 99-90327

1ST TRADE PAPER PRINTING JANUARY 2000

BACK PHOTO TAKEN BY LINDA DARKING (LADY D)
MANUFACTURED IN CANADA

Acknowledgments

Thank you Cindy Goldrick for your numerous reads and suggestions that helped to make a better book.

Thank you Jennifer Bruce and Simon Corman for listening.

BOOKS BY TERENCE MUNSEY

The BEST-SELLING STONEMAN Series™

THE FLIGHT OF THE STONEMAN'S SON
ISBN 0-9697066-0-X LCCN 93-93660
Book 1

THE KEEPER OF THREE
ISBN 0-9697066-1-8 LCCN 93-86550
Book 2

LABYRINTHS OF LIGHT
ISBN 0-9697066-2-6 LCCN 95-94007
Book 3

MARKS OF STONE
ISBN 0-9697066-3-4 LCCN 96-94015
Book 4

THEY OF OLD
ISBN 0-9697066-4-2
Book 5

MYSTERY

OBSESSION
ISBN 0-9697066-5-0 LCCN 97-92895

EMERALD CITY
ISBN 0-9697066-6-9 LCCN 98-65102

DIVE MASTER
ISBN 0-9697066-7-7 LCCN 99-70052

L.A.
ISBN 0-9697066-9-3

NON-FICTION

HOW TO: BE A PUBLISHED AUTHOR
ISBN 0-9685152-0-7 LCCN 99-90327

Available at your bookstore or our website.

AUTHOR'S NOTE

HOW TO: BE A PUBLISHED AUTHOR came about as a result of the many questions I get from people while I am on the road doing book signings. I am often asked if there is a simple, easy-to-read book giving a quick overview of the process of writing, publishing and selling your own book. It seems that no one has written a concise HOW TO book on this subject. Most of the HOW TO books are much longer and involved. The people I meet want something that they can read in a couple of hours. They want something that covers the basics involved, something that assists them in making a decision as to whether or not they are willing, ready or able to publish their own book.

That is the purpose of this HOW TO book, but it also lists extremely valuable names, addresses and Internet access to the most important information you need to know. Most books on the subject of independent publishing are not Internet access up-to-date. This one is. You will be able to research right away, twenty-four hours a day, in greater depth and access most of the forms and details you need, without wasting time waiting for traditional requests and responses made via mail during normal business hours.

All of this information is available at your fingertips without having to leave the comfort of your home. If you decide to travel the route of being your own publisher, this book gives you the basic information you need to know to get started very inexpensively. I have spent years and thousands of dollars acquiring the information presented here.

Whatever you do, be aware that you need to find appropriate professionals and representatives that can help you in your particular situation. The publishing industry changes every day and you will have to adjust to the changes. Resultantly, neither the publisher nor I are responsible for actions taken by readers emanating from the contents of this book.

I wish you success on your adventure. Don't forget to send me a sample of your finished book.

Terence Munsey

For late-breaking information and updates to the Appendix visit the website:

http://www.pathcom.com/~munsey

CONTENTS

Knowledge is the greatest wealth.

1

Getting Started

Process and Passion

So where do you begin? You are a person who enjoys or has a passion to write. So be original. Don't plagiarize someone else's writing or use some magical **formula*** just to get the job done, or you will end up with a book with which you aren't happy. Don't copy. If you are having difficulties, try to write about something you like; something you have a passion for, an interest in or knowledge of. Writing is an artistic endeavor and a very personal experience. No one can tell you if what you are writing is right or wrong.

If you are writing for personal or literary reasons then adopting a purely artistic motivation for your writing might be a satisfactory personal approach. Indeed the emphasis on this type of writing is of a personal, experiential nature, not motivated by the need to publish in the mass-market or make millions. You

* words in **bold** type are defined in the Glossary on pages 93-95.

write to please yourself without regard to sales or audience. The act of the writing is your pleasure and reward, not publication.

If your goal, however, is to make money writing, realistically it is easier in the beginning of your career to be more mercenary and to write and publish in a subject area that is less obscure, one that is already popular or established. It's easier to sell to an already established large market as opposed to creating a brand new one of your own, or writing to a small local interest group. Ultimately, however, you have to write what you write, develop a style and hone it.

Having said this, people ask me why I started to write in harder genres and not the easier ones. After a pause, I tell them I didn't have the benefit of a book like this one to guide me around the obvious hardships. I had to learn by trial and error. If I started over, I would probably begin my career writing mystery or romance novels before going into smaller niche markets. But that's all behind me now and, looking back, the niche markets I started in were under-supplied at the time. Maybe I was a writer being presented to a particular niche that was ready for new blood. Maybe it was luck? Who knows? But one piece of advice before you begin: it is generally difficult to sell fiction. It seems that fiction writers are a dime a dozen. Be aware of this fact.

Beyond mystery or romance fiction, self-help or non-fiction books are by far the easiest to market, probably because the media is more interested in promoting self-help and non-fiction topics to their audiences. Their audiences have a voracious appetite for self-help. Resultantly, it's easier to book a 10 minute interview with an 'expert' and discuss that topic, than spend 10 minutes talking about the plot of a fiction novel that the interviewer probably hasn't had time to read. Only big name fiction authors with other interests make good 'interviews'.

Regardless of my advice however, it is my experience that you will write what you write because it is an art form and you may not have control over the inspirational process. It is the nature of the craft. If you are set to follow this course, regardless of the odds against you, go ahead —it isn't totally bleak. But be aware of the added difficulties.

Some people thrive off such challenges and, if you are one of these people, the good news is that there are still many ways to carve out your own readership even in less commercial types of writing. You can still find a road to success. It may take longer, but in the end you should realize your goals.

Another type of writer is a formula writer. The people I meet who write according to some formula that they have found are an interesting group. Some of them luck-out and find moderate success, but most don't. When they're successful they are pleased but often wonder why they were successful and whether they can do it again. When they fail, they never really can figure out if it was just a bad formula or if they were a bad writer. People who write a book by a formula that isn't of their own creation find it hard to repeat that formula in their next book. I have discovered that these types of writers usually don't write an interesting read because they themselves are distanced from the prose and the creative process. But if all you want to do is write eighty thousand or so uninteresting words linked together on paper without regard to content, then be happy, because that is what you will get. On the other hand, if you want to write a book that is worth reading and selling, it is far wiser to write according to your passion, whatever that passion might be —fiction or non-fiction. You probably stand a better chance at being successful if you write from your own heart, experiences and knowledge.

For the purposes of this book, I am assuming that you have written a book that you believe is good and worth publishing. I stress that you have to rely greatly on your own instincts as to whether or not your book is 'good' or if there is a place for it in the real world. To check your instincts, give your book to someone else to evaluate who isn't a family member or a close friend and get their opinion. You might consider getting a few people to read it, weigh all their comments, then judge whether your instincts about your book were right or wrong.

If after this first step you still believe that your book is publishable, that's probably the reason you have searched out and found this guidebook. You are looking for some basic information that will make your book a reality.

The following chapters present the basic options available now that you are ready to publish.

2

Writing, Proofreading, Editing

Writing

Some people write longhand, some type, some dictate. Some people write every day all day, others once in awhile. Some for a few hours in the morning, others for a few hours at night. Some people write using the highest of high tech and others use their neighbor's old slow computer. The point of this? Everyone finds their own working rhythm and the writing will get done when it gets done. Usually people seem to spend a long time agonizing over their prose and take forever to finish whatever they start. Though there is nothing wrong with this approach, there are a few things to keep in mind.

As human beings we tend to work better when we set limits and goals for ourselves. It doesn't matter if you actually reach every goal, but it seems in setting them we get farther than we would if we just stumbled along without regard to any reasonable progress. I always remember someone telling me that you are only a writer as long as you are writing. Bearing that in mind, my suggestion is to set a schedule for yourself and stick to it. Don't allow laziness or any other thing to prevent you from accomplishing your set goals. No matter how daunting it may appear, just keep going and stick to your schedule. Even if you are not happy with what you are writing keep writing —it can always be erased or deleted. Writing is like a physical fitness program. You must commit to the program, and if you keep on exercising according to a regular schedule, gradually, sometimes even without noticing the effects, you get into good shape, and others comment on your good fortune. So set up a schedule for writing and just do it. Before you know it one page becomes two and three and four and five and...

TIP

No matter if you type or use a word processor or write by hand, remember to double space and use an inch margin on all sides. Put your name and title on every page at the top and number each page in the margin at the bottom. Use 8.5 x 11-inch paper. This will make it easier to read and proofread your manuscript.

Here's an example of a writing schedule that works for me.

Usually I come up with an idea and will do all the research for a book for a few months. This research can include general socializing with a particular group of people, discussions with professionals and skilled people within the field of my book's interest, travel to places that might be in the book, taking pictures, picking up all types of information, maps, brochures and so on. The list goes on. Once I feel that I have enough information, I come up with a title and then spend a few weeks just thinking about all the information I have gathered and how it relates to the title. Depending on the type of book you are writing this type of research and approach might not be for you, but once I have had a few weeks to mull over everything, I then decide what time is available to me and begin to set aside enough of it to create a writing schedule.

My schedule is very tight and I need to write a book a year, so I tend to set up a schedule that starts every day at six in the morning and ends around eleven a.m. I read scientific research somewhere that indicated the human mind is most creative in the early morning as opposed to later in the day. Though this may not be true for everyone, I have found it to be the case. Regardless, I get up every day and write for about four hours. I am at a point where I like to write about four thousand words a session. I set this word count as my goal. Some mornings it's less, other's it's more, but in the end I write about 25,000 words a week. So if I am aiming at a book of 100,000 words, the first rough draft is ready in about four weeks. You should probably aim for between 75,000 and 120,000 words. Don't worry. It's not as hard as it sounds, provided you set and stick to a schedule.

Normally, I set aside the months of January and February to write. I find this is a dead time of year after Christmas and there are fewer disturbances —everyone's partied out and broke. You may not be able to choose a schedule like this, but whatever your schedule is, set it, keep to it, and accomplish each writing session goal that you have set. I meet people who say they haven't got the time or couldn't write that way. That's fine, just as long as you choose a schedule that's right for you and stick to it. Remember... you are only a writer as long as you are writing. Also remember that this is meant to be something that you want and have chosen to do. No one is forcing you. If you are feeling forced, then maybe you are not yet ready to write. So don't. Wait until you are, but be realistic about the wait and what it means.

Another suggestion is not to correct your writing as you are creating it beyond very minor, obvious grammatical and spelling mistakes. Worry about the detail after you have finished each writing session. I find that only when I reach four thousand words do I quickly check my work for spelling and grammar using my word processor spellchecker. Then I leave it alone and stop the session. I will spend the rest of the time before the next scheduled writing session thinking about what I might want to write and don't worry about what I have just written. Usually if things are going okay I will have a sense that the prose is moving along well. If it isn't, I'll worry about it later at the end of the 100,000 words. It's been my experience that if you bog yourself down too much in the nitty gritty, grammatical nuts and bolts of writing during the initial creative sessions, your prose will suffer and you will become dissatisfied and stop writing. Once you stop feeling creative about what you are doing, the game is over. It's hard enough to get up and write every day without adding to the difficulties by becoming too critical of your work at the wrong stage. The initial writing is the time to let the ideas flow on to the page. Don't allow anything or anyone to deter you from your writing or your schedule. Save that for the next parts of the writing process —the proofreading and editing. That is where the real work begins. After you have finished the exciting part of putting the initial raw ideas to the page in the first rough draft, a more critical analysis of your writing is essential. At that point you have a completed 100,000-word **manuscript**, good or bad. Now you can re-arrange, correct, change and agonize over it as long as you like. The worry of finishing the first draft, of getting the foundation of your book and ideas laid, is behind you. Congratulations! You've written your first draft and are on the way to becoming a published writer.

Proofreading

That wasn't so hard, was it? Once you finish the first draft, take some time off to relax and get some distance from the prose. Proofreading is the process of checking through the manuscript for spelling and grammatical errors, missed words, incomplete sentences, paragraphing, completing thoughts, adding more flow and continuity and so on. The idea here is to catch as many mistakes as you can and add whatever you need to make the first draft better. There are many re-reads and re-writes to be done, but you should do the first proofread yourself. It is your chance to make certain that the writing says what you want it to say. You want to refine the manuscript as much as you can or are able —getting many obvious silly and minor errors corrected. These are usually small things —anything major should be caught by the others who proofread for you.

Once you have finished your re-read, you are now ready to have your manuscript proofread for errors by someone else.

> **TIP**
>
> You should get as many proof-reads as you can. The more the writing is re-read and refined the better. You don't want to waste your time or money making other people proofread something that you should have corrected. Let them do the harder, less obvious to you, proofread.

In the Appendix section at the end of this booklet you will find some names and addresses of proofreaders. If money is no concern, phone a few and find out their rates. If money is an issue, and it usually is, find an unrelated person who will either charge a token amount or do it for a couple of free dinners or drinks, or maybe you can cut their lawn or fix something for them. Who knows? Make a deal. There are all sorts of skilled people in your neighborhood with MAs or PhDs in English, though sometimes there are people who just read a lot and have an eye for catching errors. Whoever you choose, remember that they are not editing the work or commenting on whether they like it or not, they are just correcting the mistakes that you missed. As a bonus they might make comments, but that is not what you want here. Put your ego aside. Save that for the editing process. All you want is to get the basic manuscript in good shape so it can then be edited for content, flow, style, and all those things that an editor will suggest to make the writing better.

If you have to choose a relative to proofread, that's okay, but they are not always objective enough. Though they mean well, they may not give you the level of proofreading you need — sometimes other issues affect their perception of your work and lead to biased comments and criticisms. Family don't want to hurt you —they love you. Do yourself a favor and get at least one proofreader who isn't related and will be more objective.

Make sure, whoever proofreads for you, that they write their corrections and suggestions in ink in the manuscript. It's easier for you to read later when they aren't nearby to decipher what they wrote.

Once the second draft has been proofread, go over it slowly and take as much time as you need to consider all the suggestions and mistakes that the proofreader has found. Some things may need to be corrected and others may not. Proofreaders, like you, aren't perfect. Don't give up on your own abilities in terms of communicating what you wrote. Your style may bend the traditional way a certain phrase or word is presented. That's okay, but be prepared to correct those things that just aren't right in any type of artistic license.

After the second draft has been corrected, it would be wise to get another proofread. As I have said, no one is perfect. Every proofreader will miss something —something that another proofreader may not miss.

It's up to you how many times your manuscript will need to

be proofread. Once you are satisfied that it is done, your writing should be quite polished in terms of the actual nuts and bolts. Now is the time to get an edit of the actual context of the writing.

Editing

If you've gotten this far then pat yourself on the back. You've done a lot of work, and now is not the time to give up. As with proofreading, if money doesn't matter you can go to any editor's association or **freelancer** and pay them to do the job. I suppose years ago editing was done in-house by your publisher, but the competition is so strong these days you have to get your writing almost perfect before anyone will begin to seriously consider acquiring it. Once accepted, the publisher will not find that much to change.

Like everything in the arts, editing is a subjective skill. There are good and bad editors and it is very difficult to determine what you are getting until after the job is done and you've paid them. It is not their job to correct minor grammar and spelling errors —that is up to the proofreaders. It is the editor's job to study the prose and make sure it works. They are concerned that the prose flows and makes sense; that the style is acceptable. They want to make certain your book reads smoothly and is not choppy; that everything nicely and logically moves from one point to another; to make sure that descriptions are full, and dialogue realistic. It's hard to find a good editor who will work well with you and your writing. It is important that they can recognize your style and not alter it so much that even you can't see yourself in it. Again, they are not perfect and you shouldn't revere them as gods. Ultimately you are the final judge of your style and why you have written the way you do. Don't just change things because you are told to. Sometimes the proper way isn't the best way for your writing. Sometimes it is very difficult to edit your writing without destroying whatever makes it unique or stand out. Just bear this in mind when your work is being edited. You and the editor should analyze every change that is suggested, and no change should be made unless you understand and agree with it.

> **TIP**
>
> If you don't have the money to spend on a professional editor, look to your community or writers groups and, like your proofreaders, make some sort of deal with the best-qualified person you can find. In the end, any edit is better than none —though it is important to have a proper edit done by someone, somehow. There might be a retired English professor that your sister knows, or maybe an old favorite teacher. It is a place to start. Don't rush and don't give up until you find someone on your terms. I have found that a wealth of resources exists in your own backyard, but you have to dig them out.

There will be many hours of discussion and a few more drafts of your writing before it is finally finished. Money, goodwill, and your own personal deadlines determine how many more re-reads and re-edits are done. Remember that there is no such thing as a perfect book. That is what keeps authors writing — their search for perfection.

At the end of the edit I like to have one more proofread done in hopes of catching things that, even after this process, might have been missed. Again it's best to have someone else do this who hasn't read the writing yet, but realistically this is not always possible. It's hard to believe that things are missed, but it happens. I have written books that were great stories, the editing was great, but the typist or the proofreader missed things that got into print. There's no point agonizing over it. You do the best you can at the time with whatever resources are available to you, always knowing that the next writing project will be better. The important point to remember is not to let these things stop you from writing. It does get better and easier.

3

Publishing?

Publishing? What is it?

I am always amazed when I talk to people who want to be published. 'How do I get a publisher?' they ask. I am never quite sure what to say to them. I am not sure what they really want to hear. They always seem possessed and willing to give anything to be published. It's as if they believe the word has magical qualities and will somehow bestow wealth, fame and fortune upon them if only they were published. Well the truth of the matter is that anyone can get published. As for wealth, fame and fortune…that's another story. I have always made money with my writing, but it isn't by some magical process and, though it is a nice living, it's not a fortune. And what about the fame? If you are primarily interested in fame to motivate you to write, then you probably won't be writing for long. Fame is flighty and very unpredictable. Fame is not some instant occurrence. It's a by-product of hard work and determination and a lot of luck. Of course luck is defined as being able to find an opportunity and then take advantage of it.

Being published simply means that your writing is made available to the public. It should be obvious that even if your writing is made available to the public, it doesn't mean that anyone will read it, or even care about it. It's like any other new product on the market. There's no difference from the others, yet people seem to believe or want to believe that it is different. Wannabe authors only focus on the top few percent of writers —the glamorous ones living Hollywood lives —and not the vast majority of typical published writers scraping by like any other worker in any other job. Resultantly, they want to become like that small percentage right away. Hence the desire to become published —to be magically propelled into that glamorous world. Not to say that lightning doesn't strike. Sometimes it does. If you feel you are one of those very rare lucky ones I'm happy for you, but it's too chancy for me. I prefer to put my trust in the reliability of hard work and building a career, like any other job —and so should you.

'So how can I get published?' they ask again, still without realizing what they are really asking.

It seems to me that there are two choices and both of these have pros and cons.

1. Find someone to publish your book.
2. Publish it yourself.

Let's look at both of these options in more detail.

Finding someone to publish your book

There is a standard process to follow now that you have your completed manuscript.

The Literary Marketplace is probably the best source book available. Take a moment and turn to the Appendix for publication details. Most libraries keep one in their reference section. You can buy one but it changes every year and will be out of date quickly. Use the one in the library. Look up publishers and find the ones that publish your type of writing. Find out a name of someone at the publishing house to send your manuscript to. This is usually someone in the editorial department. Follow any instructions regarding submission. If there are no instructions, you have several options. You can send your finished manuscript with a cover letter to the publisher. It usually takes anywhere from one month to a year to get a response. I believe in sending out multiple inquiries.

> **TIP**
>
> If you want the manuscript returned most companies expect you to include a SASE (self-addressed stamped envelope) or they will not return it to you. Remember, publishers get thousands of manuscripts a year and it's too expensive for them to pay the return postage. Or tell them there is no need to return the manuscript. I have found that some publishers will pay for the postage and return a manuscript, but it is rare.

Or submit a cover letter and a **synopsis** of the book and a sample chapter. Some publishers prefer this approach. Again it will take a while to get a response. The Literary Marketplace will sometimes indicate the publisher's response time to submissions.

Keep sending out manuscripts or synopses until you manage to sell your manuscript or are tired of the rejections. I hope you are lucky, but don't expect much. Some of the larger publishers will receive in excess of 500 **unsolicited** manuscripts a month and thousands of general inquiries either by phone, fax, e-mail, or post. The smaller publishers will receive 20 to 50 manuscripts and/or inquiries per month. There is a lot of competition. It is very difficult for publishers to respond and keep up with the never-ending supply of unsolicited manuscripts.

In terms of copyright protection of your manuscript, if you are concerned there are many ways to protect it, but I haven't found that this is a big problem in North America. Still, there is a chance of theft. If you don't want to take any chances see the Appendix for the address of the copyright office. Write the office (or go online) and ask for the forms to register an unpublished work. The process is very straightforward and self-explanatory, and it guarantees you protection from theft of your intellectual property. The choice is yours.

Publish it yourself

People don't realize that in their quest to get published by someone else they usually give up a lot. Normally the author will get between ten and fifteen percent as a royalty and as little as five hundred to a thousand dollars advance if you're fortunate (which can be returnable if your books don't sell). If you publish your book yourself, on the other hand, you get it all. Why give away up to ninety percent just to have someone else publish your book? It doesn't make sense. You are going to work hard promoting the book trying to 'make it' and most of your hard work and efforts will go to someone else. If your book doesn't do very well —and most of them don't —it will be very difficult to convince a publisher to pick up your next book, and you're back to square one. When you consider that most books by new authors sell very low quantities (usually from 3-5000 are printed and possibly only a few hundred actually sell) and that you must work hard to build a readership and publish at least five books before you see good results, it makes sense that, at least in the early days while you are doing a lot of the ground work, you should own the material, reap the profits and publish it yourself. Moreover, you will have a better chance at building a career in publishing.

Self-publishing isn't that hard to do and it's not that expensive. Anyone who smokes and drinks regularly spends more money in a year on those activities than it costs to publish a book. Of course self-publishing can be looked down upon by some —it's a snob thing. Whenever I meet someone who looks down on self-publishers it tells me right away that they really don't understand the world of publishing, nor anything about how to be a published author who can make a living at his or her writing without having to wait on tables in a restaurant.

The rest of this book is dedicated to giving you a very quick overview of the process of becoming your own publisher and selling your books. It is designed to take the mystery out of the process without becoming a technical journal. It quickly covers the basic dos and don'ts that you need to know in order to make your book acceptable to the marketplace and book industry in terms of the minimum standards. It will start you off into the world of being a published writer just like those other published authors you've always envied. This HOW TO, is a basic guide to get you going quickly and easily on the road to making money as a published author.

4

Text and Cover

There are some basics you need to know and do if you publish your own book. You don't want to go through the process and spend the money to publish only to discover that a store won't carry your book because you forgot to put the proper **barcode** on the cover, or the proper city on the imprint page. No one will tell you about these things until it is too late. Everyone assumes you know. Follow these basics carefully. Use the checklist (see the Appendix page 91) to make sure you have done them all before you go to print.

Text and layout

The first thing to decide is the format and size of your book. You can choose from hardcover (trade), trade paper, or **mass-market** paperback formats and all levels and qualities of paper. Your decision will depend entirely on the type of book you are publishing and your budget. My suggestion is you discuss the options with your printer. Your printer can show you samples and will be very helpful. For our purposes, let's use this book as an example.

This book is set up for what is called 'trade paper' (5 1/4" x 8 1/4" trim size). The **font** used in the main text is Times 11 and the line spacing is 18 pt. The **header** is set 1/2" from the top and the **footer** 1/2" from the bottom of the page. The inside margin (closest to **binding**) is set at 5/8" from the main text to the edge. The **justification** of the text is set to 'justified' giving clean straight lines of text on every page. The outside margin is set at 1/2" from the edge. Printers like to have a little leeway, say 1/4" from the edges. Though they will work as close as 1/8" from the edge to your text, I don't recommend it.

The header is in Helvetica 10 and is in small caps (first letter is one size larger than rest). The footer is in Helvetica 7. You can number the pages any way you want. Usually page one is labeled on the first page of the actual prose and not the several pages that come before, such as the imprint page, dedication page and so on.

In this book I've started the numbering right on the imprint page (the first page of the book that displays the title and cities of publication) to make it easier to direct the reader.

You may choose to use different fonts and sizes according to what you want. If you are uncertain as to what choice to make, go to your bookstore and find other books like the one you are going to publish and make comparisons in terms of the text, its size, positioning on the page and spacing. Try to mirror the standard **layout** that is used by the industry. You don't want your book to stand out too much. Standing out sometimes confuses buyers and may hurt sales of your book.

Each genre in the book industry seems to have its own general style of layout. People have gotten used to this layout and deviating too far from it bothers them. Your book, whether good or bad, better or worse, will just seem different if you deviate too far from industry norms. If a book appears different, people will consider more carefully before they buy. I know it's crazy, but different might mean to them that your book may not be very good and they will be unwilling to buy it. They might buy the book next to yours, which may not be a great book but better fits the visual cues readers believe make a good book. Genre readers tend to be creatures of habit.

Next, you want to apply the text and layout decisions you've made to your manuscript. There are several ways to do this. You can type page by page and manually set it up, or set it up in a word processing program. Manual set up is an expensive way to publish since it is very labor intensive for the printer and you end up paying for that extra work. The best way is to use a page layout program. There are two or three really good ones. I use **Quark**, but you should use the one you prefer or have access to. Remember that most printers want page counts in multiples of eight. It's just the way their machines are set up. Make sure your final document is a multiple of eight. Add a blank page or two to ensure this works out.

By laying the text out in a layout program you can take advantage of digital processing, which substantially lowers the printing cost. This is because the printer can print directly from your digital file-to-press with minor set up costs as compared to the traditional **film-to-plate** process that many printers still use. Whatever the type of book you are publishing, the end result is crisper and cleaner if you use the digital process. This is particularly true if you are including any images on the pages.

Once you have laid out the text, it is important to get a proof-read to be certain that everything has ended up the way it should. You don't want any surprises after your book has been printed. There are also some things that you must include in the text. See the chapter 'Some Requirements' and make certain to note the requirements and place them in your book.

If you are copying the text layout from a book that you found in the bookstore, just keep comparing the book with the formatting on your word processor or page layout application. It will take several attempts but you should be able to closely approximate the layout if you are patient and persistent. Whatever you do, take your time to come up with a nice professional looking result.

Cover

Though you can't judge a book by its cover, most people do. The cover is the single most important selling feature of your book, aside from you being in the store with it in person. It is important to take your time to create a cover that stands out and at the same time fits the industry standard for your genre. If you aren't very artistic, seek out a friend and get them to design a cover for you. Of course you can hire a professional to do this. —It will cost about $2000 by the time you're finished. You can decide, depending on the availability of money, how to do your cover. If you decide to do the design yourself, spend a lot of time in the bookstore comparing covers before you start.

Once you are ready, there are a couple of things to do. The first is to phone the printer you plan to use and ask how big the **spine** should be for the number of pages in your book. Also ask them the **specifications** for the cover and what they prefer to be given. I find most want at least 1/4" beyond the trim size to work with. Since they do trim the book, give them at least 1/4" to work with. They need some place to cut without ruining the cover art. They will be able to give you exact cover specifications. This will allow you to set up the cover precisely.

When setting up the cover there are a couple of methods to use: the old way and the digital. The old way requires that you manually make all the **separations** and the printer films them and sets up the plates. This is a more expensive method again because of the labor involved, and the results aren't as good. Digital, as discussed earlier under text layout, is really the way to go. You can use one of the layout programs as you did with the text —again, I prefer Quark but there are quite a few others on the market. Check with any computer programs retailer.

On this book the trim size (final size after cutting) is 5 1/4" x 8 1/4" with a spine of 1/4". When I set up this cover in Quark I

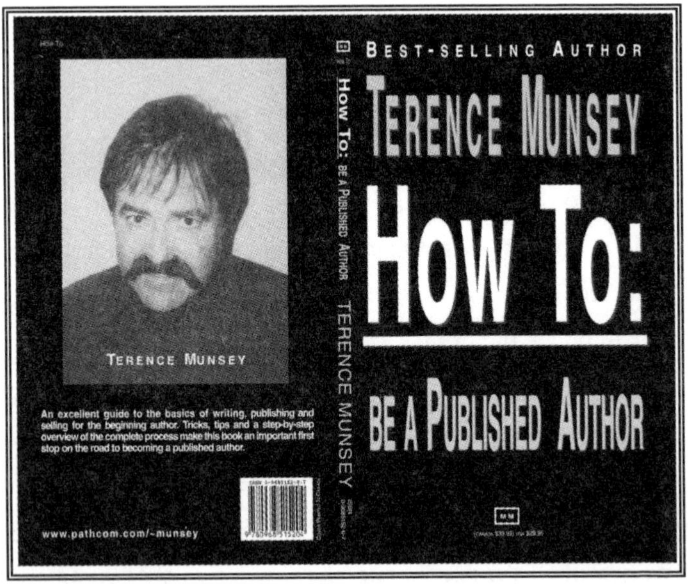

added 1/4" all round and started with a rectangle of the whole **cover flat** (front-spine-back) that measured 11 1/4" x 8.75". It should look something like the cover flat above.

This is a very simple cover. The background is black. The title has a shadow effect. The spine text has been rotated to fit vertically. All the text was manipulated through my layout program until it looked the way I wanted it. You can do anything you want. The picture is a digital file. The barcode is also a digital file. I would give this completed cover file and all the image files used to the printer. With digital processing, what you see is what you get.

That's the process, but there are some requirements to include on both your cover and text. The next chapter deals with these requirements and briefly explains why they are necessary.

5

Some Requirements

There are certain things that you need to include in your text and on your cover if you want to sell your book or register it with certain agencies. It's important to do these things before the book is printed. Though I suggest that you request information by writing, the faster and better way is to go to this book's Appendix then visit the websites of the various agencies listed and get or request the information online. In most cases, everything you need to know or want to ask is available online —even the forms. If you aren't able to go online use the regular postal system, but it will take much longer.

Let's start with the text and work our way through. Note that normally there would be no page number on the imprint page (page 1). Nor would you put a number on pages 2 through 10 nor 92, nor 96, of this book. This has been done because of the nature of this guide book. It makes it easier for you to understand and follow.

Imprint page

(page 1)

This is the very first page of your book after you open the cover (see page 1). This page is required by the industry, and identifies the publication by title, author, publisher and country(s) of publication. In order to list with certain agencies, it is required. If you want to list in a different country such as the United States or Great Britain and you don't include the appropriate information on the imprint page you may have difficulties and will be regarded as a foreigner to their industry. You don't want to reprint an entire book because you forgot to put a city of publication on the imprint page. So just include it and avoid later problems and cost.

Copyright page

(page 2)

The next page (see page 2) is the copyright page. This page, which should follow the imprint page, carries all the notices that are required both by law and for your own personal security. MAKE SURE YOU HAVE ALL THE INFORMATION YOU NEED ON THIS PAGE BEFORE THE BOOK IS SENT TO BE PRINTED. The copyright page consists of several items:

Disclaimer

You need to protect yourself against lawsuits from people who might claim that they are a character in your book and have been libeled, or people who might sue you after reading your book and blame you for any misfortunes that may happen to them. Depending on the type of book you are publishing you need to use the appropriate disclaimer. The best thing is to get a lawyer to write one for you but, if you don't want to spend the money, check out several books in the bookstore in your market and read their disclaimers. From the ones you read come up with something that works for your book.

Title and publisher address

Somewhere on the copyright page you should put the title and the name of the publisher (that's you). Don't forget to include the mailing address and any phone, fax, e-mail or website addresses. All these things help to generate sales. By prominently displaying your address information it makes it very easy for people to find you to order books. If you haven't set up a name / company, do it and register it with the appropriate governmental agency. You will need to set up a small business. Most people start with a sole proprietorship, which is the cheapest and fastest way to go, while some set up a limited company. There are many pros and cons to each. Talk to a couple of your friends who run their own businesses and have them help you understand the different types of businesses you can set up. When you are ready to register, call you local provincial or state government agency. They can tell you what to do. It is a very quick and simple process.

Copyright notice

You must not forget to register the copyright in your book. The registration process is done after the book is printed and made available to the public for sale. In the Appendix you will find the addresses for the Canadian and United States copyright offices.

In Canada contact the copyright office to request the forms for registering a published literary work. They will send you a package that explains everything (or go to their website — everything is explained online). Fill out the form and pay the fee and follow the submission requirements. The fees change but they are currently around $80CAN. Check the website for up-to-date pricing.

For United States copyright, contact the copyright office and request Form TX and a copyright information package. Fill out Form TX and follow the submission requirements. The fees change but they are in the $25US range. Check the website for up-to-date pricing and online forms.

You can register with both Canada and US or just one. I tend to register with both. Regardless of where you register, you must include the universal copyright notification © followed by year and owner to secure international protection. It is also wise to include a paragraph such as the one on page 2. Feel free to copy it. This must be on your copyright page. Don't forget it. MAKE SURE YOU HAVE ALL THE INFORMATION YOU NEED BEFORE THE BOOK IS PRINTED. The information you receive from the respective copyright offices will explain all the requirements.

Lost or stolen

This simply protects you from paying twice on returns and notifies the public that the book must be in complete condition with a cover when they purchase it or it is a book that was reported as stripped and destroyed for return. Yes, some people try to return your book for credit by returning the cover (which is a common enough practice) and then resell the remaining part without the cover (this is illegal). Though it doesn't happen often, it is smart to include such a notification —you never know.

Cataloguing in Publication (CIP)

This is a voluntary program between publishers and libraries. Its purpose is to catalogue books before they are published, and to distribute this catalogue to libraries and booksellers. Of course, this makes it easier to sell more of your books. In a sense it is free advertising. Many libraries will see an advance notice of publication of your book and order it. The library market is very lucrative. CIP is a very good program to participant in. Contact the CIP office in your jurisdiction. If you live in Canada contact the National Library. If you live in the United States contact the CIP / Copyright Office (see the Appendix for contact information). They are very helpful and will answer all your questions. They will issue your CIP information. Put it in your book exactly as they direct (see page 2 for example). You will also need a Library of Congress Catalogue Number if you want U.S. libraries to order your book. It's free, so take advantage of it.

Library of Congress Catalogue Number

If you want to take part in this program make sure there is a U.S. place of publication on the imprint page as well as a Canadian, or you won't qualify. This program pre-assigns a Library of Congress Catalogue Number (LCCN). This number identifies your book and is issued for books that may be added to the Library of Congress collection or other agencies. It facilitates cataloguing and other book processing activities that libraries and agencies might use to list your book. It boosts sales to be listed in as many places as a possible, particularly where libraries and suppliers to libraries are concerned.

Printing history

List here the printing history of your book. It is common practice. It helps to identify the particular edition of the book. These dates can be projected. For example, if you plan to make your book available to the public in September, but it is printed in August, list the printing date as September.

Credits

Any photographs or artwork that you might include in your book, either on the cover or in the text, should be credited here. This is done not just as a courtesy to those who have provided a service to you and have not required any fees —it is also important to identify the owner and designer of the cover art and any photographs. If you are wondering about ownership of artwork, usually it belongs to the employer, not the employee. So if you hire someone to do the job, it comes under 'Work-for-hire' copyright laws. Check this out with a lawyer or the appropriate copyright agency if you are uncertain.

Place of manufacture

Most countries require that the place of manufacture be included on the copyright page. Without this notification your book may not be legal for sale within your own country or for transport into another country. If the book is 'Made in Canada' or 'Made in the USA' it must be so noted on the copyright page. It is the law.

That completes the Copyright page (page 2). From time to time there are changes in the law and industry, but these are the minimum standards required. Make sure you follow them all. They are all there for a good reason. —To protect you.

The order of pages that follow the Imprint and Copyright pages is up to you. In fact, you may decide not to include any other notification pages. These pages are optional and more a part of the art of book making and publishing. I like to include them as a warm up for the reader to gain more information on the book. Sometimes it helps to put certain pages in to give the book the right look and feel. Remember that the odd pages will be on top (the right-hand side) and the even pages underneath (the left-hand side). You might add a blank page(s) (e.g. pages 8, 10) to create an attractive beginning to your book and to make sure the pages you add are situated nicely in terms of the opening of your book. It's up to you, but most good books do this and it does make for a better product. Check out other books and you'll see what I mean.

Acknowledgments

(page 3)

There are a lot of people who help you along the way as you write and publish a book. Whether the help is direct or indirect, this is the place to acknowledge their assistance. You might have a long list and include everybody, or a shorter one including the most important. You will know whom to thank and it tends to personalize your book, giving a human quality beyond the paper, ink and pages.

Other books

(page 4)

People who enjoy your writing and your book will want to know if there are any other books that you have written. This page informs the reader of everything that is available (or planned). It is a good advertisement for you. If you are planning another book in the future you should notify people here of its pending existence. That way your readership will be notified and keep an eye out for it. Try to keep this list at least one year ahead. It increases sales of the next book since there is already an awareness of it and you are not starting from scratch. No matter how small or large, there will be a budding built-in readership for subsequent books.

Author's note

(page 5)

This is the opportunity for your reader to get to know the author outside of the book. It is also an opportunity to quickly inform the reader and give them more interest in buying and reading your book. It should include some information about how and why the book was written. It can be several pages or very short. There are many variations on the theme. Sometimes it is a preface that has been written by someone else. Usually that someone else is a well-known authority or a celebrity.

Contents

(page 7)

Because this is a non-fiction HOW TO book there is a table of contents. This helps the reader find those sections that are of interest and in a way gives an outline, in heading form, of the book. This is a requirement for this type of book. If you are writing fiction there is no need for a table of contents, but you can include one if you like.

Dedication page

(page 9)

Sometimes a quote or a saying or just a remembrance of a loved one is placed here. It is a permanent marker for all to read. You should think of adding one if you feel it is appropriate.

About the author page

(page 92)

At the end of the book some publishers insert a short paragraph or two about the author. This usually includes such information as where the author lives and who the author is in terms of nationality, education or social status. It is a way to end your book on a personal note. Look at a few samples and decide what you want to say, but keep it brief and to the point.

Last chance page

(page 96)

That's what I call the very last page of the book. It is the final chance to inform the reader of other books or give information about the publisher. At the very least you should put an address and other contact information here. Make it as easy as possible for someone to find out about your books or the publisher. It makes good business sense.

That's the basic approach as far as the requirements for the text portion of your book go. Use the information in the Appendix to make the whole process easier. There's a lot of information for you to gather and work to do, but it isn't that hard and it isn't expensive. It just requires that you spend several hours familiarizing yourself with the details. Take it one step at a time and before you know it you will have met all the requirements and included them in the appropriate places in the text portion of your book.

Once you accomplish your goals, there's just one more step to take before you are ready to print —making sure the cover is right. Yes…there are also a few requirements for the cover. Though there are not as many requirements as the text, they are equally necessary and important. Take your time and follow them all. You are almost done.

Cover requirements

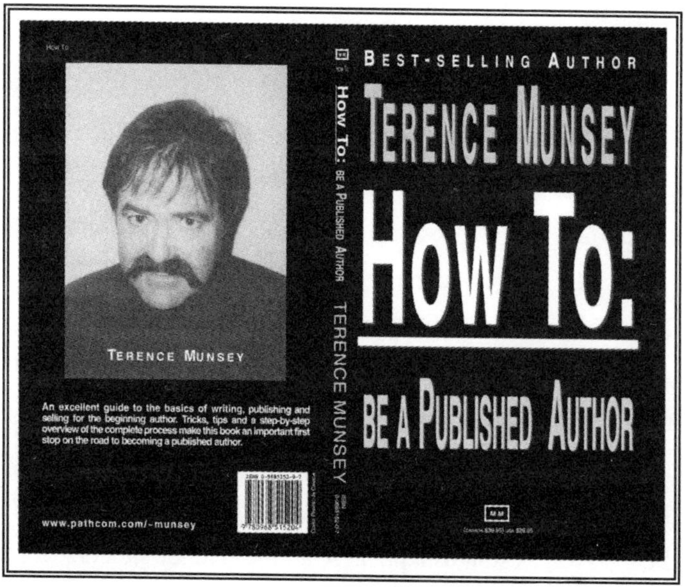

Now that the text is all laid out and you have included everything you need, let's have a look at the requirements for the cover. No matter what the final trim size of your book is going to be, the basic cover requirements are the same. Refer to the actual cover of this book if you find the diagram hard to see.

Most countries require that the publisher indicate where the cover was printed. You should place this somewhere on the back cover. In this case the notification is placed beside the barcode. You may put it anywhere. Your cover design and layout will most likely determine the spot.

Another requirement in this technological age is to place a barcode on the back cover. The barcode allows retailers and other agencies to scan the book. This makes it easier to ring up sales and inventory books. Even **distributors** require a barcode. If you don't put one on the book, it will be impossible to get your book carried by stores or distributors.

In this case the barcode is a bookland EAN price code. When it is scanned it links the book's **ISBN** to whatever information the particular agency or company has in its database. In stores, for example, they will set up their cash register to identify the book by title, price and genre.

Barcode Graphics (see Appendix) is the best place to go anywhere in North America. They are leaders in the field. Barcodes come in many shapes and sizes and are very cheap. This bookland EAN price code was e-mailed to me from the company, who made it within one hour of being ordered, and it cost under $15CDN. It was sent as a positive and was an 80 percent x 1.5" EPS Mac file. I told the barcode graphic company that I wanted a barcode for my cover that was being digitally created on a Mac computer. They asked me a few questions and then created it. When I got the **EPS file**, I merely pasted it into the position I wanted on the back cover. I have found that most books place the barcode on the bottom corner side of the back cover, though some put it on the inside back cover. I don't like the inside cover method because it adds a complication to the printing process that can cost more money. Moreover it requires the person scanning to open the cover to look for the barcode. When the barcode is clearly visible on the back it is easier to find and scan. The easier you make it for retailers to find the barcode the more likely they are to carry your book.

You can find a graphics company to create your barcode by looking in the Yellow Pages under barcode graphics. If you want to use the company I use (it can all be done by phone or e-mail), see the Appendix for contact information.

> **TIP**
> Make sure the barcode is black on a white background when you set up the cover. Barcodes seem to work best when they are black on white.

Another thing to put on the cover is the ISBN of the book. I tend to put it on the spine near the bottom, but you can place it anywhere. It is easier to find when it's on the outside cover and the book is shelved spine out.

As the publisher, you set the price of the book. (See the selling section). The price should be clearly visible either on the front or back cover in the case of a paperback, or on the inside flap of the slip cover for a hardcover. Before you decide, look at a few books in your genre in the bookstore and note what the publisher has done. Set your price to be competitive but keep your budget in mind as well. In the early days, price can be a major determining factor as to whether someone does or doesn't buy your book. If you are planning to sell the book in other countries, it is smart to put the price for that country on the book also. That way you can be certain you are getting your fair share of the actual selling price. Sellers are not allowed to charge more than your set price without your permission. Remember you have sold them the book and discounted it according to your set price. It isn't right if they turn around and sell it for more and not give you your share. (See Chapter 6 Printing and Selling.)

You should also indicate on the cover the genre to which your book belongs. For example: fiction, non-fiction, HOW TO, science fiction, biography, art. This helps the store to shelve your book appropriately. If you don't put a category designation on the cover, your book may be placed in the wrong section of the store or library. This makes it difficult not only for the reader to find, but also for the store clerk or librarian who won't know where to find it once it is shelved. This notification is usually placed on the spine in small print or on the back cover, or both places.

Though it is not a requirement, it is advisable to place endorsements and blurbs (brief explanations of the contents of the book) on the cover. These give the reader a quick overview of the book's contents and are meant to pique their interest and make them want to pickup your book. A good endorsement by a known person or organization helps. A brief but catchy blurb helps sell the book. Take your time and try to do the best you can. If you know someone who writes good promotional copy, have him or her read the book and write a compelling blurb for you. A good blurb can mean the difference between selling a lot of books easily or none at all.

Usually the blurb goes on the back cover. Endorsements can go anywhere. If it is a brief endorsement such as: 'A fabulous read!' Bob Jones, New York Times, put it right on the front cover.

Getting endorsements is hard. If you, your friends, colleagues at work, relatives, whoever, know someone famous, notable or expert in the topic covered by your book, it will be much easier. Unfortunately that may not be the case. You can try and get an advance review, but I haven't found it very easy. This is one of the cons of self-publishing. Some people and agencies in the industry will ignore you. Don't let that stop you. Do whatever you can and if you can't get an endorsement, don't worry. It's not the end of the world. Just make your blurb even more compelling.

Somewhere on the cover you should put the logo and name of the publisher. If you go to the bookstore and compare books, you will see how publishers advertise their company's name. Some put it on the spine; others put it on the front cover in small print next to the price. Some put it in both places. Remember, when your book is sitting on the shelf it might be spine out or front out. In either case it is good to have your publisher name visible.

Speaking of name and visibility, we come to the last few cover elements: the author and title of the book. These are important. You want to place them on the spine and front cover.

Obviously the front cover font size will be larger, but the spine must be clearly set up as well. If the book is spine out you want the title and author to stand out. If the cover is front-out (store-fronted), you want the title, author and cover to catch the eye of the reader. Covers do sell books. Spend a long time deciding on the appearance of the cover —on the fonts, size, colors, art-work, embossing, foil stamping (see the printing section) and so on. Once the book is printed it is too late and prohibitively expensive to make changes and corrections.

Now that you have your cover and text ready, it's time to discuss the final stages of printing and selling.

6

Printing and Selling

Printing

I assume that you are not going to attempt to print your book yourself. It would not be a wise choice if you are seriously going to compete in the major book markets. I have yet to see a homemade book that looks professional enough for the mass-market.

There are many printers in the world. I recommend that you speak with several printers. The more printers you talk to and get quotes from, the better acquainted you will become with the industry of printing. Over the years I have searched them out and compared quality with such things as text, paper, cover, binding, reliability, customer service...in short the whole package. Though you may find someone else, I have not found anyone better for customer service and professionalism than Webcom Ltd. Webcom is an international company with offices all over North America. (See their website in the Appendix.)

They can do everything for you in one place at a very competitive price. I don't think you'll do any better elsewhere, but that's up to you to decide.

As I mentioned earlier in the book, during your final layout process you will have contacted a printer to decide and get specifications for your book. You should have the layout done to those specifications. What you need to do now is get a quote for manufacturing. You will need to decide on the quantity of books and whether it will be hard or soft cover, **perfect binding** or **Otabinding**, and what quality of paper to use. Otabinding gives your paperback the look of a hardcover and is the same price as the standard perfect binding. Webcom has the exclusive rights to Otabinding. It is worth going to them just for the **binding**. Whichever company you use, the printer can help you make your layout decisions.

To a certain extent the market you are planning to sell to will determine the type of book you make. Personally, I avoid hardcover and go straight to paper. It's easier to compete in the paperback business. Also someone is more likely to pay $9 to read a new unknown general fiction author in paperback as opposed to $35 in hardcover. Moreover, the shipping and handling costs are a lot cheaper for paperback than hardcover.

The one advantage to manufacturing hardcover is that libraries prefer and tend to order and catalogue hardcover books over paperbacks. If your primary sales are intended to be in stores, I suggest publishing paperbacks, but it will depend on your particular circumstances.

Some printers will send you information sheets about book manufacturing. Here's a sample Webcom Ltd. Quotation. Prices and details will vary according to your specific needs.

WEBCOM
books and beyond

QUOTATION

Webcom Limited
3480 Pharmacy Avenue
Toronto, Ontario
Canada M1W 2S7
Tel: (416) 496-1000
(800) 665-9322
Fax: (416) 496-1537
E-mail: webcom@webcomlink.cor
Web site: www.webcomlink.com

Customer
Publishing Company
123 Main St.
Anytown, ON

Date:	July 28, 1999
Representative:	Bob Smith
Reference No:	ABC
Re:	Budget Book

BASIC SPECIFICATIONS

Quantity:	1,000/2,000/3,000 / Add'l 1000's
Finished Size:	5 ¼ x 8 ¼ (no bleeds on text pages)
Material Supplied:	Application Files (text and cover)
Text Pages:	256
Ink:	Black
Paper:	55lb Trade Book White
Cover Ink:	4/0
Cover Paper:	10ptC1S
Other:	Layflat Gloss Film Lamination
Binding:	Perfect Bound
Shipping:	Pack in standard cartons Deliver Toronto ON, one lot.

SCHEDULE Based on 20 working day turnaround from receipt of all supplied components; with 48 hour proof approval and minimal changes.

Terms: TBC

PRICE

1,000 Copies @	$X.XX/copy
2,000 Copies @	$X.XX/copy
3,000 Copies @	$X.XX/copy
Add'l Copies @	$X.XX/copy

Visit our new Web Site at www.webcomlink.com

PLEASE NOTE

Please see reverse for conditions of sale. All authors alterations and extra work will be charged at our standard prices. Cost of changes will not be confirmed unless specifically requested. Price of paper will be as market at the time of delivery. This quotation is valid for 30 days from date of issue.

Per: ______________________

Sales Representative

WEBCOM Sales offices in Canada and USA

Assuming you print paperback, I would suggest printing somewhere between three and five thousand books. If you go hardcover, print about two thousand books. Though your quantity will be determined by price, get quotes on quantities of 1000, 2000, 3000, 4000, and 5000. That way you can see the price differences and any potential savings. The unit price per book decreases with each increase in quantity printed.

When you request a quote, supply the printer with the following information: hard or soft cover; the color processing (four color or spot) and artwork for the cover; paper quality, **page count** (in multiples of eight); and any other significant specifications that will influence the final quote. The printer will be very helpful and work through the process with you. Take a printed color copy of your proposed cover with you to show them. Also take a printed copy of the completed text layout. It helps to physically see the layout. Ask the printer about **smear proofing**, or **UV** (ultra violet) **coating**, or **lay flat lamination** or any other options they might suggest for cover and text. They will even show you samples to help you make your choices.

There are some initial costs (non-recurring costs) that you don't pay again if you reprint provided you don't make any changes. Every time you change something there is a per item charge. It doesn't take long for these to pile up and become very expensive.

There is a cover set up cost anywhere between $100 and $350 depending on the cover. If you decide to have the front cover and spine title and author name embossed and gold, silver, brass or bronze foil stamped (this is the process where the letters are raised up and covered with actual gold, silver, brass, or bronze foil), the cost of the cover will be slightly more expensive, but it isn't a big difference and it does help sell the book. It is a nice look and I recommend it. Foil stamping and embossing the spine works better with Otabinding. Consider stretching your budget to include foil stamping and embossing —you won't regret it.

There is also the initial text set up cost, which is determined by the number of pages. It also depends on whether there are pictures or diagrams on the pages. If your file is comprised digitally of three hundred pages of plain text it will be between $600 and $900. If you reprint you won't be charged this set up cost again.

The printer will give you a unit price based on the quantity you want to manufacture, adding in the extra few cents per copy to foil stamp, etc. He will also give you a lower price for any copies over the main order. It is hard to stop the presses right on the exact number you order. If you tell the printer that you will accept overs, they will probably ship a hundred or so books over the order and charge a nominal amount between fifty cents and a dollar each for those extra copies. It is up to you whether or not you are willing to accept overs.

Usually the books are priced-out on a twenty-day turnaround and include one shipping. In other words the books will be ready and shipped to you in about four weeks at no extra charge. If you are willing to give the printer a longer turn-around time, you can get a discount. It's worth considering if you aren't in a rush. You should also arrange payment terms with the printer. All of the above will be included on the one page quote. Remember it is best to meet and get quotes from at least three printers. Take what you learn from each visit and use that information when negotiating with another. This way you'll get a fair price. But don't always assume the lowest quote is the best. Go with the printer who combines fair price with good service and gives you a sense of security that they will perform to the standard you expect.

> **TIP**
>
> I always ask for 90 to 120 days, but they may only be willing to give you 30 days. The amount of time you get depends on your own business negotiation skills.

Once you decide what and how many books to print, when you want to start the job, and when you want to take delivery, you will give all your final set up text and cover files, including a color print-out of the actual cover and a copy of final text, to the printer. They will then begin to process your book.

Within a week the printer will ship **proofs** of the cover and text to you to examine and either approve or send back for corrections. They will also return all the files and copies of the cover and text that you gave them. Check the proofs well. Remember, if you find a mistake they made, they pay to correct it. If you find a mistake you made, you pay to correct it. It is important that the files you deliver to the printer are perfect in terms of the final output.

When you get the proofs you will be given a couple of days to go over them and then return them with either your approval or a list of corrections to be made. Although it is unlikely that there will be any errors, it's up to you to carefully check and read everything. Look for obvious marks and make certain that everything is where it should be. If you have any questions, phone and talk to the printer. Once you sign-off and return the proofs the book will be put on schedule to be printed and whatever you approved will be the end result. So take your time and be very careful.

> **TIP**
>
> One last thing to note. Let the printer know where the books are to be delivered and that he is to call when they are ready for delivery. At delivery time you will be more aware of any special shipping needs. For example if they are being shipped to your home you will have to tell the printer that you don't have a docking bay and so they should deliver the skids of books using the appropriate truck. This saves everyone a lot of time and energy.

If you've made it this far you've done a lot of hard work. There are about four weeks before your books are delivered. Make sure you have readied a protected dry space in which to store them. Before you sit back and catch your breath, fill out the Advance Book Information form to get some advance notice to the book industry of your book being published (see R. R. Bowker website). Since this is your first book, you may have missed the Books In Print and Forthcoming Books deadlines for the current listings. Usually I notify them six months ahead of publication so there is a listing of my title in the year that it is published. Even if everything isn't completed it is important to list early and project as accurately as possible publication information.

Now you can sit back for a short rest. The real job of publishing is about to begin.

Selling

It is very unusual for anything to happen overnight. If you talk to most overnight successes you will quickly discover that overnight means a background of years of hard work. The three things that all successful people have in common are:

1. They keep trying.

2. They go just a millimeter farther in everything they attempt than the unsuccessful person. If you apply yourself and stay with it, you will be successful.

3. The most important characteristic that separates the successful person from the failing one is luck. Remember our definition? *The ability to find an opportunity and then take advantage of it*. When it comes to your book this is your challenge: find opportunities to exploit your book and take advantage of them.

There is no one way to sell your book. The successful publisher will work just a millimeter harder to find a way to build a market for it. Most people seem to think that just because your book is in a store you have it made and everything will look after itself. Well that isn't true and it doesn't look after itself. It is a constant struggle that brings, with every extra millimeter, greater rewards. I meet people who bitterly complain that they haven't been able to get their book into stores. They think it will make a tremendous difference. They believe without the stores they are dead in the water and they stop trying to sell their book. 'Take off your blinders' I tell them. If you are not ready to do extensive touring (book promotions) and support the book with all sorts of media and advertising, it isn't necessarily wise to jump into the stores. Stores want to know that you have and will implement a plan to aggressively market your product. If a demand is created for your books the stores will beg to have them. If there is no demand they won't give you the time of day. Stores return books that don't sell within a couple of months. It's a lot of work and expense for them. So getting a book into a store only to have it returned isn't very smart. Bookstores won't be interested in buying another product from you in the future. Just remember this when you start calling on the buyers in stores. Have a plan and be very professional. How much luck you have is totally dependent upon your business acumen. It takes time and a plan. DON'T GIVE UP!

When you do sell your book to stores you usually discount the cover price. The industry standard is 40 percent, but save that for your best customers. Do whatever you can to place the books in stores, but be prepared to support the product extensively once you do.

There are other areas where you can start marketing your book as well. Join the Publisher's Marketing Association

(PMA) and get involved in their library and school mailings. This will generate orders. These orders can be filled directly by the publisher or you can take advance of the services of Baker and Taylor, or Ingram Books (multi-faceted book industry companies that, amongst their services, can act as a distributor and/or a **fulfillment** warehouse for your book) to make it easier for libraries who may deal exclusively with these companies, to buy your book once they see it advertised through the PMA mailings.

You should also set up arrangements with distributors like John Coutts (a supplier to libraries) or Jack the Bookman or any other distributors who will buy some of your books to sell to their customers. Remember that in Canada and the USA libraries set aside funds to buy books from authors of their own nationality. So there is an advantage in letting Canadian customers know you're a Canadian author, and likewise if you're an American author in the United States. Track down as many agencies in your country that are mandated to buy domestic titles. For example: military libraries, prisons, and specialty stores that deal in your book's topic.

Other places to get listed are the Internet bookstores. It's easy to sign up with them. Online shopping is a rapidly increasing segment of the marketplace in books. Don't overlook this important market. When your book starts selling it is a natural transition for online stores to want your book on the shelf in their physical bookstore.

Book fairs are also a great way to generate both sales and

attention. Go to as many as possible. You will make sales and contacts that will lead you to other opportunities.

Of course don't forget your friends. Sell a book to every one of them. Don't give them away. Your friends should want to support you and help you get going. The only free promotional copies should be saved for legitimate opportunities such as publicity. You will find that approximately 2 to 3 percent of your books will be given away as promotional samples in the hopes of getting interviewed on radio, TV or national newspapers. Also seek out community cable TV and local newspapers. Get them to do stories on you. Donate some books to charity in return for publicity opportunities.

> **TIP**
> One good agency that will help you get radio and television interviews is Bradley Communications. Unfortunately they prefer to take on non-fiction. So if you've written fiction they won't be of much help. Fiction is a much harder marketplace to sell to.

Your job as publisher is to find and make as many opportunities for your book as possible. To dig up leads anyway you can. To find and use every connection you have. You might hire a publicist to arrange a media tour, or set up a book signing tour yourself, or act as your own publicist. It's not easy, but it isn't impossible. Just keep working away at it. Join the ABA (American Booksellers Association) or the CBA (Canadian Booksellers Association). Join any and every association that will help you to make contacts and sell your book. (See Appendix for publicists). Start small and work your way up. Every sale you make is one book closer to being a best-selling author. I did it and, believe me, if I can do it, anyone can.

There are endless opportunities out there. This section has given you a few good places to start, but there is much more to be exploited. It's your job to find those opportunities.

Now that you are well on the road to selling your book, make sure to set yourself attainable goals and targets. More importantly, achieve them. It doesn't take long to build a readership, provided you give a constant effort. These are the types of things you would be doing if someone else published your book. It's part of the job description. The only difference is that you are not sharing the sales profits: you keep all the money for yourself. So get out there and sell, sell, sell!

7

Last Few Things to Do

Once your printed books arrive there are several things to do after the book is published (made available to the public). They are presented in checklist format. Check them off as you complete them.

__Complete US Copyright Application form TX and send required deposit copies.

__Complete Canadian Copyright Application form and send.

__Send required legal deposit (CIP) copies to National Library in Ottawa, Canada.

__Send required deposit copies to LCCN / CIP in US Copyright office.

__Send one copy to The US Gift Exchange.

__Register your book with Books in Print USA.

__Register your book with Books In Print Canada.

__Send out a press release announcing your publication.

(Make your own list, hire a publicist, or get addresses online.)

8
Congratulations

If you were lucky you managed to make arrangements for the stores to carry your book while you were waiting for it to be printed, and their initial order has covered all your costs. If not, you are working on them as well as all the other opportunities out there. Regardless, you are selling your book and people are reading it. You will be doing book signings and making other appearances. In fact your readers are looking forward to your next book.

Send me a copy for my collection:
Box 511
Richmond Hill, Ontario
L4C 4Y8

Congratulations! You are a published author. All your efforts have paid off and you are on the road to a new career.

APPENDIX

Proofreading and Editing

If you haven't been able to find someone through word of mouth or by asking other writers or writers groups, try your local university or college or school (preferably in their English or Communications department) and ask them if anyone is available to proofread. If that brings no success look up editor or editorial and proofreading services in the phonebook. If that doesn't work search the Net using "editorial service+your state". It will bring up about fifty sites. It's a hard choice, but in the early stages, when money is tight, I recommend finding someone local as suggested in the section on proofreading. You don't always get what you pay for. Be careful. For more help contact:

CANADA
Editors' Association of Canada
35 Spadina Road
Toronto, Ontario
Phone: 416-975-1379
Fax: 416-975-1839
E-mail: eacinfo@web.net
Website: http://www.web.net/eac-acr

USA
Editorial Freelancers Association
71 West 23rd Street, Suite 1504
New York, NY
10010-4102
Phone: 212-929-5400
Fax: 212-929-5439

Copyright, CIP, ISBN, LCCN, Legal Deposit

Canadian Copyright Office

Canadian Intellectual Property Office
Industry Canada
Place De Portage 1
50 Victoria Street, Second Floor
Ottawa, Ontario
K1A 0C9
Phone: 819-997-1936
Fax: 819-953-7620
E-mail: cipo.contact@ic.gc.ca
Website: http://cipo.gc.ca

Canadian CIP Office

CIP OFFICE
National Library of Canada
395 Wellington Street
Ottawa, Ontario
K1A 0N4
Phone: 819-994-6881
Fax: 819-997-7517
Email: cip@nlc-bnc.ca
Website: http://www.nlc-bnc.ca/cip/e-cip.htm

Canadian ISBN

Canadian ISBN Agency
National Library of Canada
395 Wellington Street
Ottawa, Ontario
K1A 0N4
Phone: 819-994-6872
Fax: 819-997-7517
E-mail: isbn@nlc-bnc.ca
Website: http://www.nlc-bnc.ca/services/e-isbn.htm

Canadian Legal Deposit

Canadian Acquisitions and Legal Deposit Office
National Library of Canada
395 Wellington Street
Ottawa, Ontario
K1A 0N4
Phone: 819-997-9565
Fax: 819-953-8508
E-mail: legal.deposit@nlc-bnc.ca
Website:
http://www.nlc-bnc.ca/services/e1legal.htm

ISBN
819-994-6872

United States Copyright Office

Library of Congress
The Copyright Office
101 Independence Avenue S. E.
Washington DC
20559-6000
Phone: 202-707-3000
Fax-on-demand: 202-707-2600
E-mail: copyinfo@loc.gov
Website: http://www.loc.gov/copyright

United States CIP Office

Library of Congress
CIP Division
COLL/CIP (4320)
Washington DC
20450-4320
Website: gopher://marvel.loc.gov/11/services/publishers/cip

United States ISBN

R. R. Bowker
121 Chanlon Road
New Providence, NJ
07974
Phone: 908-665-6770
Fax: 908-665-2895
Website: http://www.bowker.com/standards/home

Library of Congress Catalogue Number

Library of Congress
The Copyright Office
CIP and LCCN Division
101 Independence Avenue S E
Washington DC
20559-6000
Phone: 202 707 5000
Fax-on-demand: 202-707-2600
E-mail: copyinfo@loc.gov
Website: http://lcweb2.loc.gov/pcn/

Gift Exchange

The Library of Congress
Exchange and Gift Division
Gift Section
Washington DC
20540-4200

Chain Bookstores

Canada

Chapters
90 Ronson Drive
Toronto, Ontario
M9W 1C1
Phone: 416-243-3132
Online bookstore: http://www.chapters.ca

Indigo Books & Music
82 St. Regis Crescent
Toronto, Ontario
M3J 1Z3
Phone: 888-446-3446
Online bookstore: http://www.indigo.ca

United States

Amazon.com Books
Catalog Dept., PO BOX 80727
Seattle, Washington
98101-0727
Phone: 206-346-2952
Fax: 206-622-2100
E-mail: catalog-dept@amazon.com
Online bookstore: http://www.amazon.com

Barnes and Noble,
122 Fifth Avenue, 4th Floor
New York, NY
10011
Phone: 212-633-3300
Online bookstore: http://www.barnesandnoble.com

Borders Group, Inc. (includes Walden Books)
500 E Washington Street
Ann Arbor, MI
48104
Phone: 734-477-1100
Fax: 734-913-1965
Website: http://www.bordersgroupinc.com
Online bookstore: http://www.borders.com

Barcode

Barcode Graphics Inc.
30 Dohme Avenue
Toronto, Ontario
M4B 3M4
Phone: 416-751-1474
Fax: 416-751-1575
E-mail: orders@barcodegraphics.com
Website: http://www.barcodegraphics.com

Printers

Webcom Ltd.
3480 Pharmacy Avenue
Toronto, Ontario
M1W 2S7
Toll Free: 1-800-665-9322
Phone: 416-496-1000
Fax: 416-496-1537
E-mail: webcom@webcomlink.com
Website: http://www.webcomlink.com

BookMasters Inc.
2541 Ashland Road
PO Box 2139
Mansfield, OH
44905
Toll Free: 800-537-6727
Phone: 419-589-5100
Fax: 419-589-4040
E-mail: wires@bookmasters.com
Website: http://www.bookmasters.com

Book Fairs

An excellent website that includes a lot of information on many book fairs is listed below. Check out this site.

http://
publishing.about.com/msub18.htm?pid=2770&cob=home

Miami Book Fair International
300 N. E. 2nd Avenue, Suite 1501
Miami, FL
33132
Phone: 305:237-3258
E-mail: bookfair@mdcc.edu

Toronto Small Press Book Fair
PO Box 561, Stn P
Toronto, Ontario
M5S 2T1
E-mail: maggie@web.net

San Francisco Bay Area Book Festival
San Francisco Bay Area Book Council
123 Townsend St., Ste. 260
San Francisco, CA
94107
Phone: 415-908-2833
Fax: 415-908-2839
E-mail: festival@sfbook.org

The Word On The Street
40 Wellington St. E., 3rd Floor
Toronto, Ontario
M5E 1C7
Phone: 416-504-7241
Fax: 416-504-7656
E-mail: wotstoronto@sympatico.ca
Website: http://sites.sympatico.ca/wots

Book Distributors —Canada

Jack the Bookman
10 Newkirk Road South, Unit 16
Richmond Hill, Ontario
L4C 5S3
Phone: 905-884-6177
Fax: 905-884-2411

John Coutts Library Service Limited (USA & Canada)
6900 Kinsman Court, Box 1000
Niagara Falls, Ontario
L2E 7E7
Toll Free Phone: 800-263-1686
Phone: 905-356-6382
Fax: 905-356-5064
E-mail: coutts@wizbang.coutts.on.ca
Website: http://www.coutts-ls.com/

Christie & Christie Associates
226 Alice Street
Kincardine, Ontario
N2Z 2S5
Toll Free Phone: 800-263-1991
Toll Free Fax: 800-458-0025

Pegasus Wholesale Inc.
100 Alfred Kuehne Boulevard
Brampton, Ontario
L6T 4K4
Phone: 905-789-1234
Fax: 905-789-0695

Book Distributors —United States

Baker & Taylor
Publisher Services
44 Kirby Avenue
Somerville, NJ
08876
Toll Free Phone: 800-775-1800
Phone: 908-722-8000
Website: http://www.baker-taylor.com/

Publisher Relations Department
Ingram Book Company
One Ingram Blvd.
La Vergne, TN
37086-3629
Website: http://www.ingrambookgroup.com/Pub_Info/newpu-binfo/

Listings

Advance Book Information Form:
R. R. Bowker Data Collection Center
Box 6000
Oldsmar, FL
34677-6800
Phone: 813-855-4635
Fax: 813-855-2309
Website: http://
www.bowker.com/standards/home/isbn/us/printable/abi.html

USA and Canada
Books In Print
R. R. Bowker Data Collection Center
Box 6000
Oldsmar, FL
34677-6800
Phone: 813-855-4635
Fax: 813-855-2309
E-mail: booksinprint@bowker.com
Website: http://www.bowker.com/bip/

Canadian Books In Print
10 St Mary's Street, Suite 700
Toronto, Ontario
M4Y ZW8
Phone: 416-265-1631
Fax: 416-921-6353

Marketing

Publisher's Marketing Association
627 Aviation Way
Manhattan Beach, CA
90266
Phone: 310-372-2732
Fax: 310-374-3342
Email: info@pma-online.org
Website: http://www.pma-online.org

American Booksellers Association
828 South Broadway
Tarrytown, NY
10591
Toll Free Phone: 800-637-0037
Phone: 914-631-7800
Fax: 914-591-2720
E-mail: info@bookweb.org
Website: http://www.bookweb.org

Canadian Booksellers Association
79 Don Mills Road, Suite 700
Toronto, Ontario
M3C 1T5
Phone: 416-467-7883
Fax: 416 467 7886
E-mail: enquiries@cbabook.org
Website: http://www.cbabook.org

Chesterton Rev.
306-966-8
Brick
416-593-9684
Essays on Olde Writing
416-694-3
Lit. Review of Ida
416-532-55

www.magomania.com

Literary Reviews
Quill and Quire
905-946-0406.
Books In Canada
416-924-2777

Publicists

Publishers Weekly
245 West 17th Street
New York, NY
10011
Phone: 212-463-6758
Fax: 212-463-6631
E-mail: pw.letters.to.the.editor@bookwire.com
Website: http://www.publishersweekly.com/
http://www.publishersweekly.com/about/masthead.asp

Media-Television-Radio Interviews

Bradley Communications
135 East Plumstead Avenue
Lansdowne, PA
19050-8206
Toll Free Phone: 1-800-989-1400
Phone: 215-259-1070
Fax: 610-259-5032
E-mail: contasus@rtir.com
Website: http://www.rtir.com

News Wire Services

Canada NewsWire Ltd.
Water Park Place, Suite 914, 10 Bay Street
Toronto, Ontario
M5J 2R8
Phone: 416-863-9350
Fax: 416-863-4825
E-mail: cnw@newswire.ca
Website: http://www.newswire.ca

P R NewsWire
810 Seventh Avenue, 32nd Floor
New York, NY
22229
Phone: 1-800-776-8096
Fax: 1-800-793-9313
E-mail: nyhubs@ornewswire.com
Website: http://www.prnewswire.com

Book Reviews —Canada

Canadian Book Review Annual
44 Charles Street West, # 3205
Toronto, Ontario
M4Y 1R8
Phone: 416-961-8537
Fax: 416-961-1855
E-mail: cbra@interlog.com

CMPA (Canadian Magazine Publishers Association)*
130 Spadina Avenue, Suite 202
Toronto, Ontario
M5V 2L4
Phone: 416-504-0274
Fax: 416-504-0437
E-mail: cmpinfo@cmpa.ca
Website: http://www.cmpa.ca
*Ask for their catalogue of magazines. There is a nominal charge

Book Reviews —United States

Kirkus Reviews
200 Park Avenue South
New York, NY
10010-1543
Phone: 212-777-4554
Fax: 212-979-1352

American Library Association
Booklist
50 East Huron Street
Chicago, IL
60611
Phone: 312-944-6780
Fax: 312-337-6787
E-mail: ala@ala.org
Website: http://www.ala.org

Reference Books

Literary Market Place
Website: http://lmp.bookwire.com/lmp/us/index_us.asp

Publisher:
R. R. Bowker
121 Chanlon Road
New Providence, NJ
07974
Phone: 908-665-6770
Fax: 908-665-2895
E-mail: info@bowker.com

FORMS

1. Canadian Copyright Application Form

2. United States Copyright Application
   Form TX

Canadian Sample Copyright Application FORM

(page one)

OPIC
Office de la propriété intellectuelle du Canada

CIPO
Canadian Intellectual Property Office

Application for Registration of a Copyright

(please print)

1. Title of the work

2. Category of the work

☐ Literary ☐ Musical ☐ Artistic ☐ Dramatic ☐ Compilation

Short description of the work and/or rights being registered:

3. Publication

☐ A. The work is published ☐ B. The work is unpublished

Date of first publication: Y M D	Place of publication: City/Town (optional)	Prov./State (optional)	Country

4. Author(s) ☐ Same as owner(s) - (If more than one author, please attach a list of names and addresses of all the authors)

Family name	First name	Initial	Date of author's death, if known Y M D

Address

City/Town	Prov./State	Country	Postal/Zip Code

5. Owner(s) - (If more than one owner, please attach a list of names and addresses of all the owners)

A. Family name	First name	Initial

OR B. Name of corporation

Address

City/Town	Prov./State	Country	Postal/Zip Code

Industry Canada Industrie Canada

(000528-02-98)

Canada

Canadian Sample Copyright Application FORM

(page two)

6. Applicant(s)

A. The applicant is the same as owner in section 5. B. The applicant is the same as author in section 4.

OR

C. Family name First name Initial

OR D. Name of corporation

Address

City/Town Prov./State Country Postal/Zip Code

7. Declaration

The applicant is:

A) author(s) B) owner(s) C) assignee(s) D) licensee(s) of the copyright in the work

8. Agent for applicant (if applicable)

A. Family name First name Initial

OR B. Name of firm

Address

City/Town Prov./State Country Postal/Zip Code

Telephone no. Fax no. (if available) E-mail address (if available)

( ) ( )

(For Canadian Intellectual Property Office use only)

All correspondence should be addressed to:

Canadian Intellectual Property Office
Copyright Office
Place du Portage I
50 Victoria Street
Hull, Quebec K1A 0C9
Telephone: (819) 997-1725, Facsimile: (819) 997-6357
Internet address: http://cipo.gc.ca

Please do not send copies of your work

U.S. Sample Copyright Application FORM

(page one)

FEE CHANGES
Registration filing fees are effective through June 30, 1999. For information on the fee changes, write the Copyright Office, check http://www.loc.gov/copyright, or call (202) 707-3000. Beginning as early as January 1, 2000, the Copyright Office may impose a service charge when insufficient fees are received.

FORM TX
For a Nondramatic Literary Work
UNITED STATES COPYRIGHT OFFICE

REGISTRATION NUMBER

TX TXU

EFFECTIVE DATE OF REGISTRATION

Month Day Year

DO NOT WRITE ABOVE THIS LINE. IF YOU NEED MORE SPACE, USE A SEPARATE CONTINUATION SHEET.

1

TITLE OF THIS WORK ▼

PREVIOUS OR ALTERNATIVE TITLES ▼

PUBLICATION AS A CONTRIBUTION If this work was published as a contribution to a periodical, serial, or collection, give information about the collective work in which the contribution appeared. Title of Collective Work ▼

If published in a periodical or serial give: Volume ▼ Number ▼ Issue Date ▼ On Pages ▼

2

a NAME OF AUTHOR ▼

DATES OF BIRTH AND DEATH
Year Born ▼ Year Died ▼

Was this contribution to the work a "work made for hire"?
☐ Yes
☐ No

AUTHOR'S NATIONALITY OR DOMICILE
Name of Country
OR { Citizen of ▶
Domiciled in ▶

WAS THIS AUTHOR'S CONTRIBUTION TO THE WORK
Anonymous? ☐ Yes ☐ No
Pseudonymous? ☐ Yes ☐ No
If the answer to either of these questions is "Yes," see detailed instructions.

NATURE OF AUTHORSHIP Briefly describe nature of material created by this author in which copyright is claimed. ▼

NOTE

Under the law, the "author" of a "work made for hire" is generally the employer, not the employee (see instructions). For any part of this work that was "made for hire" check "Yes" in the space provided, give the employer (or other person for whom the work was prepared) as "Author" of that part, and leave the space for dates of birth and death blank.

b NAME OF AUTHOR ▼

DATES OF BIRTH AND DEATH
Year Born ▼ Year Died ▼

Was this contribution to the work a "work made for hire"?
☐ Yes
☐ No

AUTHOR'S NATIONALITY OR DOMICILE
Name of Country
OR { Citizen of ▶
Domiciled in ▶

WAS THIS AUTHOR'S CONTRIBUTION TO THE WORK
Anonymous? ☐ Yes ☐ No
Pseudonymous? ☐ Yes ☐ No
If the answer to either of these questions is "Yes," see detailed instructions.

NATURE OF AUTHORSHIP Briefly describe nature of material created by this author in which copyright is claimed. ▼

c NAME OF AUTHOR ▼

DATES OF BIRTH AND DEATH
Year Born ▼ Year Died ▼

Was this contribution to the work a "work made for hire"?
☐ Yes
☐ No

AUTHOR'S NATIONALITY OR DOMICILE
Name of Country
OR { Citizen of ▶
Domiciled in ▶

WAS THIS AUTHOR'S CONTRIBUTION TO THE WORK
Anonymous? ☐ Yes ☐ No
Pseudonymous? ☐ Yes ☐ No
If the answer to either of these questions is "Yes," see detailed instructions.

NATURE OF AUTHORSHIP Briefly describe nature of material created by this author in which copyright is claimed. ▼

3

a YEAR IN WHICH CREATION OF THIS WORK WAS COMPLETED This information must be given in all cases. ◀ Year

b DATE AND NATION OF FIRST PUBLICATION OF THIS PARTICULAR WORK Complete this information ONLY if this work has been published. Month ▶ Day ▶ Year ▶ ◀ N

4

See instructions before completing this space.

COPYRIGHT CLAIMANT(S) Name and address must be given even if the claimant is the same as the author given in space 2. ▼

TRANSFER If the claimant(s) named here in space 4 is (are) different from the author(s) named in space 2, give a brief statement of how the claimant(s) obtained ownership of the copyright. ▼

DO NOT WRITE HERE OFFICE USE ONLY
APPLICATION RECEIVED
ONE DEPOSIT RECEIVED
TWO DEPOSITS RECEIVED
FUNDS RECEIVED

MORE ON BACK ▶ • Complete all applicable spaces (numbers 5-9) on the reverse side of this page. • See detailed instructions. • Sign the form at line 8.

DO NOT WRITE H
Page 1 of ____ p

U.S. Sample Copyright Application FORM

(page two)

EXAMINED BY ______________________ **FORM TX**

CHECKED BY

☐ CORRESPONDENCE Yes

FOR COPYRIGHT OFFICE USE ONLY

DO NOT WRITE ABOVE THIS LINE. IF YOU NEED MORE SPACE, USE A SEPARATE CONTINUATION SHEET.

5

PREVIOUS REGISTRATION Has registration for this work, or for an earlier version of this work, already been made in the Copyright Office?

☐ **Yes** ☐ **No** If your answer is "Yes," why is another registration being sought? (Check appropriate box.) ▼

a. ☐ This is the first published edition of a work previously registered in unpublished form.

b. ☐ This is the first application submitted by this author as copyright claimant.

c. ☐ This is a changed version of the work, as shown by space 6 on this application.

If your answer is "Yes," give: **Previous Registration Number** ▼ **Year of Registration** ▼

6

DERIVATIVE WORK OR COMPILATION

a **Preexisting Material** Identify any preexisting work or works that this work is based on or incorporates. ▼

b **Material Added to This Work** Give a brief, general statement of the material that has been added to this work and in which copyright is claimed. ▼

See instructions before completing this space.

7

DEPOSIT ACCOUNT If the registration fee is to be charged to a Deposit Account established in the Copyright Office, give name and number of Account.

a Name ▼ **Account Number** ▼

b **CORRESPONDENCE** Give name and address to which correspondence about this application should be sent. Name/Address/Apt/City/State/ZIP ▼

Area code and daytime telephone number ▶ Fax number ▶

Email ▶

8

CERTIFICATION* I, the undersigned, hereby certify that I am the

Check only one ▶
- ☐ author
- ☐ other copyright claimant
- ☐ owner of exclusive right(s)
- ☐ authorized agent of ______________________

Name of author or other copyright claimant, or owner of exclusive right(s) ▲

of the work identified in this application and that the statements made by me in this application are correct to the best of my knowledge.

Typed or printed name and date ▼ If this application gives a date of publication in space 3, do not sign and submit it before that date.

Date ▶

Handwritten signature (X) ▼

X ______________________________

The filing fee of $20.00 is effective through June 30, 1999. After that date, please write the Copyright Office, check the Copyright Office Website at http://www.loc.gov/copyright, or call (202) 707-3000 for the latest fee information.

9

Mail certificate to:

Certificate will be mailed in window envelope

Name ▼

Number/Street/Apt ▼

City/State/ZIP ▼

YOU MUST:
- Complete all necessary spaces
- Sign your application in space 8

SEND ALL 3 ELEMENTS IN THE SAME PACKAGE

1. Application form
2. Nonrefundable filing fee in check or money order payable to *Register of Copyrights*
3. Deposit material

MAIL TO:

Library of Congress
Copyright Office
101 Independence Avenue, S.E.
Washington, D.C. 20559-6000

*17 U.S.C. § 506(e): Any person who knowingly makes a false representation of a material fact in the application for copyright registration provided for by section 409, or in any written statement filed in connection with the application, shall be fined not more than $2,500.

December 1998—65,000 PRINTED ON RECYCLED PAPER ☆U.S. GOVERNMENT PRINTING OFFICE: 1998-454-879/80,050

Checklist

TEXT

__Notify Advance Book Information
__Check text and cover specifications
__Imprint page
__Copyright notification
__Include CIP notification
__Include LCCN notification
__Disclaimer
__Title, author, publisher, address and e-mail
__Lost / stolen notification
__Print history
__Credits
__Place of manufacture
__Acknowledgments
__Other books notification
__Author's note or preface
__Contents (if required)
__Dedication page
__About the author (end of book)
__Last chance page
__Other

COVER

__Bar code
__Cover printing location
__Publisher and logo
__ISBN
__Price
__Genre
__Endorsements
__Blurbs
__Other

About the author

Terence Munsey lives near Toronto, Ontario. He holds an MA degree from Stanford University in California. He writes fiction, non-fiction and science fiction.

Visit the website: www.pathcom.com/~munsey.

Glossary

BARCODE
A scanable product identifier used for retail packaging.

BINDING
The manner in which sections of a book are bound or held together.

COVER FLAT
The complete layout of the cover of a book as it lies on one sheet of flat paper before it is bound to a book.

DISTRIBUTOR
A company that for a fee distributes books to stores and other organizations interested in purchasing them.

EPS FILE
Short for Encapsulated Postscript File. An object-oriented file format, which maintains extreme accuracy of the object and is used for high end PostScript systems. EPS files can be color separated.

FILM-TO-PLATE
The process by which documents are transferred from regular filmed images to plates that can be used to print.

FONT
The style of type used by computer word processors.

FOOTER
A text box beyond the main text at the bottom of the page usually displaying the page number.

FORMULA FICTION
The formulated outline that is used to write a book that follows a predetermined pattern or plan and is supposedly universal for that particular genre of the writing.

FREELANCER
Someone who offers their services outside and independent from the control of any organization.

FULFILLMENT
The services offered by a company for a fee to warehouse, take orders and ship your books to any purchaser.

HEADER
A text box beyond the main text at the top of the page usually displaying the title of the book and the name of the author.

ISBN
International Standard Book Number. A unique worldwide numbering system that identifies a book. No other book will have the same number.

JUSTIFICATION
The positioning of text on a page, can be centered, left, right or justified (equal on both margins).

LAYOUT
The manner in which artwork and text is placed on a page.

LAY FLAT LAMINATION
A process used by book printers to prevent the cover from curling.

MANUSCRIPT
The unpublished handwritten or typed copy of a literary work of an author.

MASS-MARKET
The average main stream of the marketplace. The vast majority of purchasers.

OTABINDING
A method of binding that allows the cover not to be permanently attached, permitting a book to lie open and flat.

PAGE COUNT
The number of pages in a work.

PERFECT BINDING
A method of binding that permanently attaches the spine of a book to its cover.

PROOFS
A testing print of a cover and text of a book used for correction or examination before the final printing.

QUARK
Is short for QuarkXpress, a page layout application that is a registered trademark of Quark Inc.

SEPARATIONS
The various layers of text, color and artwork as broken done by color and presented separately.

SPECIFICATIONS
The measurements and dimensions of a book, including its cover and text layout.

SMEAR PROOFING
A smudge resistant coating applied to a book cover.

SPINE
The portion of the binding of a book in-between the front and back cover.

SYNOPSIS
A brief summary of the contents of a book.

UNSOLICITED
A submission that is sent without being asked for.

UV COATING
A veneer that protects the cover of a book from the damage of ultra violet radiation.

READ THESE BOOKS BY TERENCE MUNSEY

The FLIGHT of the STONEMAN'S SON $_{1}$

The KEEPER of THREE $_{1}$

LABYRINTHS of LIGHT $_{1}$

MARKS of STONE $_{2}$

THEY of OLD $_{5}$

OBSESSION $_{2}$

EMERALD CITY $_{3}$

DIVE MASTER $_{4}$

L.A. $_{5}$

HOW TO: BE A PUBLISHED AUTHOR $_{6}$

Ask your bookstore to order, or order directly from

MUNSEY MUSIC

BOX 511 RICHMOND HILL ONTARIO CANADA L4C 4Y8
E-MAIL: munsey@pathcom.com
WEBSITE: www.pathcom.com/~munsey

Please add $6.00 shipping and handling for one book. For additional books per same order add $1.00 each.

1 = $5.99 Canada ($4.99 U.S.)
2 = $6.99 Canada ($5.99 U.S.)
3 = $7.99 Canada ($6.99 U.S.)
4 = $8.99 Canada ($7.99 U.S.)
5 = $10.99 Canada ($9.99 U.S.)
6 = $39.95 Canada ($29.95 U.S.)

We try to maintain prices but prices are subject to change without notice. Mail and website orders allow 14 days delivery.